This book belongs to

PROJECT AND EVENT PLANNER JOURNAL
A Journal to Success

By Angela C Williams

This journal is specially designed to help you plan and keep track of your projects and events for the span of 12 months. Its unique design allows you to record multiple project and event ideas, highlights of each, items required, as well as to do lists and contacts required. This journal will provide you with structured writing space to successfully plan and track your projects and events.

ISBN 978-0-6151-5833-4

TABLE OF CONTENTS

Section	Page(s)
Various Project/Event Ideas	4-6
Individual Project Highlights	7, 15, 23, 31, 39, 47, 55, 63, 71, 79, 87, 95
Individual Project/Event Items Required	8-10, 16-18, 24-26, 32-34, 40-42, 48-50, 56-58, 64-66, 72-74, 80-82, 88-90, 96-98
Individual Project To Do Items	11, 19, 27, 35, 43, 51, 59, 67, 75, 83, 91, 99
Scheduler	12-14, 20-22, 28-30, 36-38, 44-46, 52-54, 60-62, 68-70, 76-78, 84-86, 92-94, 100-102

Various Project/Event Ideas	Target Date

Various Project/Event Ideas	Target Date

Various Project/Event Ideas	Target Date

Project/Event Name:

Theme/Purpose:

Project/Event Highlights

Project/Event Items Required	√	Project/Event Items Required	√

Project/Event Items Required	√	Project/Event Items Required	√

Project/Event Items Required	√	Project/Event Items Required	√

To Do Items	Due Date	Participants/Assignees

Date/Time	Day	Contact	To Do
	Sunday:		
	Monday:		
	Tuesday:		
	Wednesday:		
	Thursday:		
	Friday:		
	Saturday:		
	Sunday:		
	Monday:		
	Tuesday:		
	Wednesday:		
	Thursday:		
	Friday:		
	Saturday:		

Date/Time	Day	Contact	To Do
	Sunday:		
	Monday:		
	Tuesday:		
	Wednesday:		
	Thursday:		
	Friday:		
	Saturday:		
	Sunday:		
	Monday:		
	Tuesday:		
	Wednesday:		
	Thursday:		
	Friday:		
	Saturday:		

Date/Time	Day	Contact	To Do
	Sunday:		
	Monday:		
	Tuesday:		
	Wednesday:		
	Thursday:		
	Friday:		
	Saturday:		
	Sunday:		
	Monday:		
	Tuesday:		
	Wednesday:		
	Thursday:		
	Friday:		
	Saturday:		

Project/Event Name:

Theme/Purpose:

Project/Event Highlights

Project/Event Items Required	√	Project/Event Items Required	√

Project/Event Items Required	√	Project/Event Items Required	√

Project/Event Items Required	√	Project/Event Items Required	√

To Do Items	Due Date	Participants/Assignees

Date/Time	Day	Contact	To Do
	Sunday:		
	Monday:		
	Tuesday:		
	Wednesday:		
	Thursday:		
	Friday:		
	Saturday:		
	Sunday:		
	Monday:		
	Tuesday:		
	Wednesday:		
	Thursday:		
	Friday:		
	Saturday:		

Date/Time	Day	Contact	To Do
	Sunday:		
	Monday:		
	Tuesday:		
	Wednesday:		
	Thursday:		
	Friday:		
	Saturday:		
	Sunday:		
	Monday:		
	Tuesday:		
	Wednesday:		
	Thursday:		
	Friday:		
	Saturday:		

Date/Time	Day	Contact	To Do
	Sunday:		
	Monday:		
	Tuesday:		
	Wednesday:		
	Thursday:		
	Friday:		
	Saturday:		
	Sunday:		
	Monday:		
	Tuesday:		
	Wednesday:		
	Thursday:		
	Friday:		
	Saturday:		

Project/Event Name:

Theme/Purpose:

Project/Event Highlights

Project/Event Items Required	√	Project/Event Items Required	√

Project/Event Items Required	√	Project/Event Items Required	√

Project/Event Items Required	√	Project/Event Items Required	√

To Do Items	Due Date	Participants/Assignees

Date/Time	Day	Contact	To Do
	Sunday:		
	Monday:		
	Tuesday:		
	Wednesday:		
	Thursday:		
	Friday:		
	Saturday:		
	Sunday:		
	Monday:		
	Tuesday:		
	Wednesday:		
	Thursday:		
	Friday:		
	Saturday:		

Date/Time	Day	Contact	To Do
	Sunday:		
	Monday:		
	Tuesday:		
	Wednesday:		
	Thursday:		
	Friday:		
	Saturday:		
	Sunday:		
	Monday:		
	Tuesday:		
	Wednesday:		
	Thursday:		
	Friday:		
	Saturday:		

Date/Time	Day	Contact	To Do
	Sunday:		
	Monday:		
	Tuesday:		
	Wednesday:		
	Thursday:		
	Friday:		
	Saturday:		
	Sunday:		
	Monday:		
	Tuesday:		
	Wednesday:		
	Thursday:		
	Friday:		
	Saturday:		

Project/Event Name:

Theme/Purpose:

Project/Event Highlights

Project/Event Items Required	√	Project/Event Items Required	√

Project/Event Items Required	√	Project/Event Items Required	√

Project/Event Items Required	√	Project/Event Items Required	√

To Do Items	Due Date	Participants/Assignees

Date/Time	Day	Contact	To Do
	Sunday:		
	Monday:		
	Tuesday:		
	Wednesday:		
	Thursday:		
	Friday:		
	Saturday:		
	Sunday:		
	Monday:		
	Tuesday:		
	Wednesday:		
	Thursday:		
	Friday:		
	Saturday:		

Date/Time	Day	Contact	To Do
	Sunday:		
	Monday:		
	Tuesday:		
	Wednesday:		
	Thursday:		
	Friday:		
	Saturday:		
	Sunday:		
	Monday:		
	Tuesday:		
	Wednesday:		
	Thursday:		
	Friday:		
	Saturday:		

Date/Time	Day	Contact	To Do
	Sunday:		
	Monday:		
	Tuesday:		
	Wednesday:		
	Thursday:		
	Friday:		
	Saturday:		
	Sunday:		
	Monday:		
	Tuesday:		
	Wednesday:		
	Thursday:		
	Friday:		
	Saturday:		

Project/Event Name:

Theme/Purpose:

Project/Event Highlights

Project/Event Items Required	√	Project/Event Items Required	√

Project/Event Items Required	√	Project/Event Items Required	√

Project/Event Items Required	√	Project/Event Items Required	√

To Do Items	Due Date	Participants/Assignees

Date/Time	Day	Contact	To Do
	Sunday:		
	Monday:		
	Tuesday:		
	Wednesday:		
	Thursday:		
	Friday:		
	Saturday:		
	Sunday:		
	Monday:		
	Tuesday:		
	Wednesday:		
	Thursday:		
	Friday:		
	Saturday:		

Date/Time	Day	Contact	To Do
	Sunday:		
	Monday:		
	Tuesday:		
	Wednesday:		
	Thursday:		
	Friday:		
	Saturday:		
	Sunday:		
	Monday:		
	Tuesday:		
	Wednesday:		
	Thursday:		
	Friday:		
	Saturday:		

Date/Time	Day	Contact	To Do
	Sunday:		
	Monday:		
	Tuesday:		
	Wednesday:		
	Thursday:		
	Friday:		
	Saturday:		
	Sunday:		
	Monday:		
	Tuesday:		
	Wednesday:		
	Thursday:		
	Friday:		
	Saturday:		

Project/Event Name:

Theme/Purpose:

Project/Event Highlights

Project/Event Items Required	√	Project/Event Items Required	√

Project/Event Items Required	√	Project/Event Items Required	√

Project/Event Items Required	√	Project/Event Items Required	√

To Do Items	Due Date	Participants/Assignees

Date/Time	Day	Contact	To Do
	Sunday:		
	Monday:		
	Tuesday:		
	Wednesday:		
	Thursday:		
	Friday:		
	Saturday:		
	Sunday:		
	Monday:		
	Tuesday:		
	Wednesday:		
	Thursday:		
	Friday:		
	Saturday:		

Date/Time	Day	Contact	To Do
	Sunday:		
	Monday:		
	Tuesday:		
	Wednesday:		
	Thursday:		
	Friday:		
	Saturday:		
	Sunday:		
	Monday:		
	Tuesday:		
	Wednesday:		
	Thursday:		
	Friday:		
	Saturday:		

Date/Time	Day	Contact	To Do
	Sunday:		
	Monday:		
	Tuesday:		
	Wednesday:		
	Thursday:		
	Friday:		
	Saturday:		
	Sunday:		
	Monday:		
	Tuesday:		
	Wednesday:		
	Thursday:		
	Friday:		
	Saturday:		

Project/Event Name:

Theme/Purpose:

Project/Event Highlights

Project/Event Items Required	√	Project/Event Items Required	√

Project/Event Items Required	√	Project/Event Items Required	√

Project/Event Items Required	√	Project/Event Items Required	√

To Do Items	Due Date	Participants/Assignees

Date/Time	Day	Contact	To Do
	Sunday:		
	Monday:		
	Tuesday:		
	Wednesday:		
	Thursday:		
	Friday:		
	Saturday:		
	Sunday:		
	Monday:		
	Tuesday:		
	Wednesday:		
	Thursday:		
	Friday:		
	Saturday:		

Date/Time	Day	Contact	To Do
	Sunday:		
	Monday:		
	Tuesday:		
	Wednesday:		
	Thursday:		
	Friday:		
	Saturday:		
	Sunday:		
	Monday:		
	Tuesday:		
	Wednesday:		
	Thursday:		
	Friday:		
	Saturday:		

Date/Time	Day	Contact	To Do
	Sunday:		
	Monday:		
	Tuesday:		
	Wednesday:		
	Thursday:		
	Friday:		
	Saturday:		
	Sunday:		
	Monday:		
	Tuesday:		
	Wednesday:		
	Thursday:		
	Friday:		
	Saturday:		

Project/Event Name:

Theme/Purpose:

Project/Event Highlights

Project/Event Items Required	√	Project/Event Items Required	√

Project/Event Items Required	√	Project/Event Items Required	√

Project/Event Items Required	√	Project/Event Items Required	√

To Do Items	Due Date	Participants/Assignees

Date/Time	Day	Contact	To Do
	Sunday:		
	Monday:		
	Tuesday:		
	Wednesday:		
	Thursday:		
	Friday:		
	Saturday:		
	Sunday:		
	Monday:		
	Tuesday:		
	Wednesday:		
	Thursday:		
	Friday:		
	Saturday:		

Date/Time	Day	Contact	To Do
	Sunday:		
	Monday:		
	Tuesday:		
	Wednesday:		
	Thursday:		
	Friday:		
	Saturday:		
	Sunday:		
	Monday:		
	Tuesday:		
	Wednesday:		
	Thursday:		
	Friday:		
	Saturday:		

Date/Time	Day	Contact	To Do
	Sunday:		
	Monday:		
	Tuesday:		
	Wednesday:		
	Thursday:		
	Friday:		
	Saturday:		
	Sunday:		
	Monday:		
	Tuesday:		
	Wednesday:		
	Thursday:		
	Friday:		
	Saturday:		

Project/Event Name:

Theme/Purpose:

Project/Event Highlights

Project/Event Items Required	√	Project/Event Items Required	√

Project/Event Items Required	√	Project/Event Items Required	√

Project/Event Items Required	√	Project/Event Items Required	√

To Do Items	Due Date	Participants/Assignees

Date/Time	Day	Contact	To Do
	Sunday:		
	Monday:		
	Tuesday:		
	Wednesday:		
	Thursday:		
	Friday:		
	Saturday:		
	Sunday:		
	Monday:		
	Tuesday:		
	Wednesday:		
	Thursday:		
	Friday:		
	Saturday:		

Date/Time	Day	Contact	To Do
	Sunday:		
	Monday:		
	Tuesday:		
	Wednesday:		
	Thursday:		
	Friday:		
	Saturday:		
	Sunday:		
	Monday:		
	Tuesday:		
	Wednesday:		
	Thursday:		
	Friday:		
	Saturday:		

Date/Time	Day	Contact	To Do
	Sunday:		
	Monday:		
	Tuesday:		
	Wednesday:		
	Thursday:		
	Friday:		
	Saturday:		
	Sunday:		
	Monday:		
	Tuesday:		
	Wednesday:		
	Thursday:		
	Friday:		
	Saturday:		

Project/Event Name:

Theme/Purpose:

Project/Event Highlights

Project/Event Items Required	√	Project/Event Items Required	√

Project/Event Items Required	√	Project/Event Items Required	√

Project/Event Items Required	√	Project/Event Items Required	√

To Do Items	Due Date	Participants/Assignees

Date/Time	Day	Contact	To Do
	Sunday:		
	Monday:		
	Tuesday:		
	Wednesday:		
	Thursday:		
	Friday:		
	Saturday:		
	Sunday:		
	Monday:		
	Tuesday:		
	Wednesday:		
	Thursday:		
	Friday:		
	Saturday:		

Date/Time	Day	Contact	To Do
	Sunday:		
	Monday:		
	Tuesday:		
	Wednesday:		
	Thursday:		
	Friday:		
	Saturday:		
	Sunday:		
	Monday:		
	Tuesday:		
	Wednesday:		
	Thursday:		
	Friday:		
	Saturday:		

Date/Time	Day	Contact	To Do
	Sunday:		
	Monday:		
	Tuesday:		
	Wednesday:		
	Thursday:		
	Friday:		
	Saturday:		
	Sunday:		
	Monday:		
	Tuesday:		
	Wednesday:		
	Thursday:		
	Friday:		
	Saturday:		

Project/Event Name:

Theme/Purpose:

Project/Event Highlights

Project/Event Items Required	√	Project/Event Items Required	√

Project/Event Items Required	√	Project/Event Items Required	√

Project/Event Items Required	√	Project/Event Items Required	√

To Do Items	Due Date	Participants/Assignees

Date/Time	Day	Contact	To Do
	Sunday:		
	Monday:		
	Tuesday:		
	Wednesday:		
	Thursday:		
	Friday:		
	Saturday:		
	Sunday:		
	Monday:		
	Tuesday:		
	Wednesday:		
	Thursday:		
	Friday:		
	Saturday:		

Date/Time	Day	Contact	To Do
	Sunday:		
	Monday:		
	Tuesday:		
	Wednesday:		
	Thursday:		
	Friday:		
	Saturday:		
	Sunday:		
	Monday:		
	Tuesday:		
	Wednesday:		
	Thursday:		
	Friday:		
	Saturday:		

Date/Time	Day	Contact	To Do
	Sunday:		
	Monday:		
	Tuesday:		
	Wednesday:		
	Thursday:		
	Friday:		
	Saturday:		
	Sunday:		
	Monday:		
	Tuesday:		
	Wednesday:		
	Thursday:		
	Friday:		
	Saturday:		

Project/Event Name:

Theme/Purpose:

Project/Event Highlights

Project/Event Items Required	√	Project/Event Items Required	√

Project/Event Items Required	√	Project/Event Items Required	√

Project/Event Items Required	√	Project/Event Items Required	√

To Do Items	Due Date	Participants/Assignees

Date/Time	Day	Contact	To Do
	Sunday:		
	Monday:		
	Tuesday:		
	Wednesday:		
	Thursday:		
	Friday:		
	Saturday:		
	Sunday:		
	Monday:		
	Tuesday:		
	Wednesday:		
	Thursday:		
	Friday:		
	Saturday:		

Date/Time	Day	Contact	To Do
	Sunday:		
	Monday:		
	Tuesday:		
	Wednesday:		
	Thursday:		
	Friday:		
	Saturday:		
	Sunday:		
	Monday:		
	Tuesday:		
	Wednesday:		
	Thursday:		
	Friday:		
	Saturday:		

Date/Time	Day	Contact	To Do
	Sunday:		
	Monday:		
	Tuesday:		
	Wednesday:		
	Thursday:		
	Friday:		
	Saturday:		
	Sunday:		
	Monday:		
	Tuesday:		
	Wednesday:		
	Thursday:		
	Friday:		
	Saturday:		

Printed in the United States
137444LV00001B/17/A